Four Corners

Jack C. Richards · David Bohlke

with Kathryn O'Dell

Workbook

CAMBRIDGE
UNIVERSITY PRESS

University Printing House, Cambridge CB2 8BS, United Kingdom

One Liberty Plaza, 20th Floor, New York, NY 10006, USA

477 Williamstown Road, Port Melbourne, VIC 3207, Australia

314–321, 3rd Floor, Plot 3, Splendor Forum, Jasola District Centre, New Delhi – 110025, India

79 Anson Road, #06–04/06, Singapore 079906

Cambridge University Press is part of the University of Cambridge.

It furthers the University's mission by disseminating knowledge in the pursuit of
education, learning and research at the highest international levels of excellence.

www.cambridge.org
Information on this title: www.cambridge.org/9780521127509

© Cambridge University Press 2011

This publication is in copyright. Subject to statutory exception
and to the provisions of relevant collective licensing agreements,
no reproduction of any part may take place without the written
permission of Cambridge University Press.

First published 2011

Reprinted 2018

Printed in Italy by Rotolito S.p.A.

A catalogue record for this publication is available from the British Library

ISBN	978-0-521-12753-0	Student's Book 3A with Self-study CD-ROM
ISBN	978-0-521-12754-7	Student's Book 3B with Self-study CD-ROM
ISBN	978-0-521-12748-6	Workbook 3A
ISBN	978-0-521-12750-9	Workbook 3B
ISBN	978-0-521-12747-9	Teacher's Edition 3 with Assessment Audio CD / CD-ROM
ISBN	978-0-521-12743-1	Class Audio CDs 3
ISBN	978-0-521-12712-7	Classware 3
ISBN	978-0-521-12740-0	DVD 3

Additional resources for this publication at www.cambridge.org/fourcorners

Cambridge University Press has no responsibility for the persistence or accuracy
of URLs for external or third-party internet websites referred to in this publication,
and does not guarantee that any content on such websites is, or will remain,
accurate or appropriate. Information regarding prices, travel timetables, and other
factual information given in this work is correct at the time of first printing but
Cambridge University Press does not guarantee the accuracy of such information
thereafter.

Art direction, book design, photo research, and layout services: Adventure House, NYC

Contents

7 Personalities 49

8 The environment 57

9 Realtionships 65

10 Living your life 73

11 Music 81

12 On vacation 89

Credits

Illustration credits

Kveta Jelinek: 62, 73; Andrew Joyner: 50; Greg Paprocki: 55, 70, 77; Garry Parsons: 49, 71; Maria Rabinky: 93; Rob Schuster: 76; Richard Williams: 68, 75

Photography credits

6 ©Gulf Images/Alamy; 8 ©Media Bakery; 11 ©Juice Images/Alamy; 16 ©Michele Falzone/Alamy; 17 (*clockwise from top left*) ©Eva Mueller/Getty Images; ©Steve Gorton/Getty Images; ©Zee/Alamy; ©RT Images/Alamy; ©Shutterstock; ©Deco/Alamy; ©Siri Stafford/Getty Images; ©Ghislain & Marie David de Lossy/Getty Images; 18 ©Three Lions/Getty Images; 20 (*top to bottom*) ©Shutterstock; ©Kirsty McLaren/Alamy; 23 ©Stockbyte/Getty Images; 24 (*top to bottom*) ©Hulton Archive/Getty Images; ©Archive Photos/Getty Images; ©Ryan Miller/Getty Images; 26 ©Media Bakery; 28 ©Dreamstime; 30 (*top to bottom*) ©Media Bakery; ©Image Broker/Alamy; 32 ©Tyler Stableford/Aurora/Getty Images; 34 ©winhorse/iStock/Getty Images Plus/Getty Images; 35 (*left to right*) ©Hisham Ibrahim/Getty Images; ©Laura Ciapponi/Getty Images; 37 (*clockwise from top left*) ©Media Bakery; ©Paul Souders/Getty Images; ©Altrendo Travel/Getty Images; ©Achim Thomae/Moment/Getty Images; ©Shutterstock; ©Oliver Strewe/Getty Images; 38 ©Media Bakery; 39 ©Image Makers/Getty Images; 40 (*left to right*) ©Doug Armand/Getty Images; ©Steve Bloom Images/Alamy; ©Philip & Karen Smith/Getty Images; 41 ©Ty Milford/Getty Images; 48 (*top to bottom*) ©jossdim/Getty images; ©walterbilotta/iStock/Getty Images Plus/Getty Images; ©Jack Hollingsworth/Getty Images; ©Jeffrey Coolidge/Getty Images; 51 ©Mike Powell/Getty Images; 52 (*top to bottom*) ©Iain Masterton/Alamy; ©CSA Images/Printstock Collection/Getty Images; ©Charles Stirling/Alamy; ©Oleksiy Maksymenko/Alamy; 57 (*clockwise from top left*) ©Franz Aberham/Getty Images; ©Marlene Ford/Alamy; ©Franz Aberham/Getty Images; 60 ©Alamy; 61 (*clockwise from top left*) ©Justin Prenton/Alamy; ©Martin Leigh/Getty Images; ©Media Bakery; ©Media Bakery; ©Design Pics Inc/Alamy; ©Media Bakery; 63 (*top to bottom*) ©Fuse/Getty Images; ©Media Bakery; ©Fancy/Alamy; ©Media Bakery; ©Media Bakery; ©Media Bakery; 64 ©Media BakeryJose Luis Pelaez Inc/Blend Images/Getty Images; 69 ©Media Bakery; 74 ©Tomás del Amo/Alamy; 79 (*left to right*) ©Ian Miles – Flashpoint Pictures/Alamy; ©Magdalena Rehova/Alamy; ©Media Bakery; (*bottom*) ©Tyler Stableford/Getty Images; 82 ©Ethan Miller/Getty Images Entertainment/Getty Images; 84 ©Frederick Bass/Getty Images; 87 ©Jason LaVeris/Getty Images; 89 (*clockwise from top left*) ©Jay Reilly/Getty Images; ©Media Bakery; ©Wendy Connett/Alamy; ©Alamy; 90 ©Nicolas Russell/Getty Images; 92 ©Photo Edit; 94 ©Alamy; 96 (*left to right*) ©Ersler Dmitry/Getty images; ©Devonyu/Thinkstock; ©Theo Fitzhugh/Alamy; ©Creative Crop/Getty Images; ©Creative Crop/Getty Images.

Personalities

A You're extremely curious.

1 Put the letters in the correct order to make words for personality traits.

1. i a t s m i u b o   ___ambitious___
2. b n s u b r t o   _____
3. e a c f l r u   _____
4. i o c m i t t i s p   _____
5. r s c i u u o   _____
6. o t i g u g o n   _____
7. u d s r t o n u a e v   _____
8. a i e o y n g s g   _____

2 Complete the sentences with the words for personality traits.

John sets high goals for himself. He's very ___ambitious___ (1). He's also extremely _____ (2). He loves learning about new things.

Celia is _____ (3), but she's also pretty _____ (4). She likes trying exciting sports, but she does them with attention to detail.

Gina doesn't have a job right now, but she seems OK. She always looks on the bright side, so she's _____ (5) about her future. She hardly ever worries. She's a very relaxed and _____ (6) person.

Daniel can be very _____ (7). He never changes his mind about things! But he's also very _____ (8). He's extremely friendly, so people like to be around him.

Unit 7 Lesson A 49

3 Circle the correct words to complete the conversation.

Jane: How do your children like college, Rob?

Rob: Very much, thanks. Don is **carefully** / (**extremely**) ambitious. He sets high goals for himself. You know, he wants to be a pilot.

Jane: Wow. That's great. And the others?

Rob: Well, Greg **fairly** / **really** likes college. He's **early** / **very** outgoing. He works **early** / **well** in groups, but he thinks it's difficult to work alone, and you have do that a lot in college.

Jane: Well, it's good that he likes school.

Rob: And Ken is **pretty** / **slowly** curious. He likes to learn new things, so he loves school. He's interested in many subjects, so he hasn't decided what career he wants yet.

Jane: That sounds like my son. And how's Brandon doing?

Rob: He's doing OK. He doesn't work **very** / **well** without direction, but if you tell him what to do, he does it **really** / **well**. Ken and Brandon go to the same college, so they help each other.

Jane: That's nice.

4 Rewrite the sentences to correct the mistakes in the order of the words. Sometimes there is more than one mistake in the sentence.

1. Steven and Susan are curious extremely about the new student in class.

   <u>Steven and Susan are extremely curious about the new student in class.</u>

2. Mario doesn't play well the guitar when he's nervous.

   _____

3. Tae-ho's parents are important very to him.

   _____

4. Kendra is outgoing fairly, and she makes easily new friends.

   _____

5. Pam quickly drives, but she's careful pretty.

   _____

6. Jacob slowly is moving, so he'll be late for his doctor's appointment this morning.

   _____

50   Unit 7   Lesson A

5 Look at the chart. Write sentences about Shan.

	easily	very	fairly	hard
1. make friends	✓			
2. ambitious			✓	
3. study during the week				✓
4. not stubborn		✓		
5. not work on the weekends				✓
6. outgoing		✓		
7. optimistic			✓	
8. not share her feelings	✓			

1. _Shan makes friends easily._
2. _She is_ _____
3. _____
4. _____
5. _____
6. _____
7. _____
8. _____

6 Complete the sentences so they are true for you. Use some of the adverbs from the box.

Example: _I'm pretty ambitious._ or _I'm not very ambitious._

carefully	(not) extremely	pretty	slowly
completely	fairly	quickly	(not) very
easily	hard	(not) really	well

1. I'm _____ ambitious.
2. I'm _____ serious about learning English.
3. I'm _____ optimistic about my future.
4. I make new friends _____ .
5. I'm _____ curious about math and science.
6. I work _____ when I do my homework.

Unit 7 Lesson A 51

B *In my opinion, . . .*

1 Complete the conversations with phrases from the box. Use each expression once. More than one answer is possible.

Don't you agree	Don't you think that's true	In my opinion,
Don't you think so	If you ask me,	Maybe it's just me, but I think

Olivia: Heather, what do you think of this statue?

Heather: Oh, it's very interesting. _Don't you agree_ ?
　　　　　　　　　　　　　　　　　　　　　　1

Olivia: No, not really. _____ it's ugly.
　　　　　　　　　　　　　　　　2

Olivia: And look at this painting. What do you think of it?

Heather: I like it, but it's a little weird. _____ ?
　　　　　　　　　　　　　　　　　　　　　　　　　　　3

Olivia: _____ it's pretty amazing!
　　　　　　　　　4

Olivia: Wow. Look at this. It's great! _____ ?
　　　　　　　　　　　　　　　　　　　　　　　　　　5

Heather: No, I don't. _____ it's disgusting!
　　　　　　　　　　　　　　6

2 What do you think? Complete the conversation with your own idea. Use an expression for giving an opinion.

Olivia: Hey, what do you think of this painting?

Heather: Oh, it's nice. Don't you agree?

You: _____

_____

_____

52　Unit 7　Lesson B

C We've been friends for six years.

1 Look at the dictionary definitions for personality traits. Write the correct words.

1. a _greeable_ (adj) friendly and pleasing

2. c_____ (adj) thinking of the needs of others

3. d_____ (adj) making decisions quickly

4. f_____ (adj) treating people equally or right

5. h_____ (adj) truthful

6. m_____ (adj) behaving in a responsible way

7. p_____ (adj) waiting without getting annoyed

8. r_____ (adj) doing what is expected or promised

2 Complete the sentences with the correct words for personality traits. Use the opposites of the words from Exercise 1.

1. John is sometimes _____dishonest_____. He doesn't always tell the truth.
2. Some people in the group were _____, so we didn't become friends.
3. Jack is pretty _____. He didn't come to pick me up at the airport. I had to take a taxi home.
4. Amanda is 17, but she's pretty _____. She acts like she's only 12 or 13.
5. Please don't be _____! You don't have to wait much longer. I'm almost finished.
6. Bob and I are often _____. We hardly ever make decisions quickly!
7. Peter is a very _____ and _____ person. He never thinks about other people's needs, and he doesn't treat people equally.

Unit 7 Lesson C 53

3 Complete the chart. Write the words from the box in the correct column.

✓ 2010	a few days	last night	two months
4:30	five hours	a long time	Wednesday
December	I was 18	quite a while	a year

I've lived here for . . .	I've known him since . . .
	2010

4 Look at the calendar and the information about Vanessa. Today is Saturday. Complete the sentences with *since*. Then rewrite them with *for*.

Monday	Tuesday	Wednesday	Thursday	Friday
got a new job	met Greg at work	had a blind date with Carlos	stopped talking to Greg	got sick

1. Vanessa has had a new job *since Monday* .

    Vanessa has had a new job for five days.

2. She has known Greg _____ .

    _____

3. She has known Carlos _____ .

    _____

4. She's hasn't talked to Greg _____ .

    _____

5. She's been sick _____ .

    _____

5 Write sentences with the words in parentheses. Use the present perfect with *for* or *since*.

1. (Yolanda / be / friends with Jenna / a long time)
   <u>Yolanda has been friends with Jenna for a long time.</u>

2. (I / not see / Jun / three days)
   _____

3. (I / not have / an argument with my parents / I was a kid)
   _____

4. (Tom and Melissa / be / married / three years)
   _____

5. (Matt / not eat / sushi / he was in Japan)
   _____

6. (Sandra / know / Katia / 2005)
   _____

6 Read the email. Then answer the questions. Use *for* or *since*.

Dear Uncle Henry,

How are you? I'm great! As you know, I got married a week ago! I'm sorry you couldn't come to the wedding. Can you believe that I met Julie at your son's wedding in 2001?

Julie and I are on vacation now. We got to Hawaii four days ago. It's beautiful here! Unfortunately, Julie got sick on Wednesday, so we're in the doctor's office now. We got here at 1:00 p.m., and we have to wait a little longer to see the doctor. The office is pretty busy. Julie's mother called five minutes ago, and they're talking on the phone now. Julie's going to be OK. She probably had some bad seafood.

I have to go. They say I have to turn off my computer!

Take care,

Josh

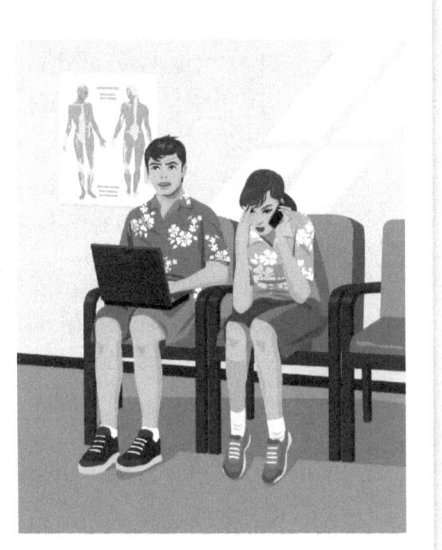

1. How long has Josh been married?   <u>He's been married for a week.</u>
2. How long has Josh known Julie?   _____
3. How long have Josh and Julie been in Hawaii? _____
4. How long has Julie been sick?   _____
5. How long have they been in the doctor's office? _____
6. How long has Julie been on the phone? _____

D What is your personality?

1 Read the article. Then answer the questions.

1. Which color in the article do you like best? _____
2. Are you like (or not like) the personality description for that color? _____

What does your favorite color say about your personality?

We all have a favorite color. But did you know that your favorite color might say something about your personality?

WHITE. White is a peaceful color. You like simple things. You are extremely fair, and you always tell the truth. You also want your friends to be truthful.

RED. Red is a strong color. You are outgoing and like meeting new people. You are optimistic and very ambitious. You are also decisive, and you are sometimes stubborn.

ORANGE. You are pretty easygoing and you like to be agreeable. You are curious about people and like to learn about them. You have a lot of friends. You want people to notice you, and you sometimes dress in flashy clothes!

YELLOW. Yellow is a happy color. You are very funny and have a lot of friends. You are pretty adventurous, too! But sometimes you are not very responsible. That's not always a bad thing because taking risks is fun if you are careful.

GREEN. Green is the color of nature. You're fairly curious about the world. You like to be outdoors, and you are also adventurous. You are patient, kind, and easygoing.

BLUE. Blue is also a color in nature. Like "green" people, you are also very patient. You are reliable, and you want your friends to be considerate. You probably aren't very adventurous.

PURPLE. Purple is a color for creative people. You like music and the arts. You enjoy visiting museums and taking pictures.

BLACK. Black is a mysterious color. You have secrets. You are very curious about many different things.

2 Read the article again. Then circle the correct word to complete each sentence.

1. People who like white are **(honest)** / **dishonest**.
2. People who like yellow **like** / **don't like** trying new things.
3. People who like red are **good** / **bad** at making decisions.
4. People who like blue probably **like** / **don't like** trying new things.
5. People who like purple are usually **creative** / **boring**.
6. People who like black often **have** / **don't have** secrets.

The environment

A Going green

1 Complete the text with one word from box A and one word from box B.

A	e-	global	hybrid	~~nuclear~~	organic	plastic	recycling	solar	wind
B	bags	bin	car	~~energy~~	energy	farm	food	warming	waste

Easy Ways You Can Help the Environment

1. Many people don't like _nuclear energy_. They prefer to get their electricity from a _____.

2. Buy and drive a _____. They don't use as much gas as other cars, and they cause less pollution.

3. Take your own cloth bags to the supermarket. Don't use _____.

4. Cook and eat _____. It is safer for the environment.

5. Regular lightbulbs are not good for the environment. Use CFLs instead. This will help reduce _____.

6. Put a large _____ in your house, and recycle paper, glass, and plastic.

7. When you buy a new computer, don't throw the old one away. If it still works, give it to a friend. This will help reduce _____.

8. Use _____ to dry your clothes. Put your towels, blouses, shirts, pants, and even jeans on a clothesline to dry in the sun.

Unit 8 Lesson A 57

2 Write C (count noun) or N (noncount noun).

1. energy __N__
2. e-waste _____
3. lightbulb _____
4. recycling bin _____
5. pollution _____
6. plastic bag _____
7. bottle _____
8. landfill _____
9. plastic _____

3 Complete the sentences with *fewer* or *less*.

1. The world would be a better place with _____less_____ e-waste.
2. People should use _____ plastic bags.
3. There should be _____ pollution in big cities.
4. There are _____ wind farms in the United States than in Europe.
5. Many people are trying to use _____ energy in their homes.
6. I'm sure you'll use _____ gas with your hybrid car.

4 Complete the letter with *too many* or *too much*.

LETTER TO THE EDITOR

June 17

I read the article *Building Goes Up Green* yesterday. It was very interesting, and I'm glad we're going to have a shopping mall that is better for the environment. There are _____too many_____ buildings in this city that are bad for the environment. Most
                        1
buildings use _____ energy, so it's important that the new
                        2
buildings will use solar energy.

I think that the mall has a lot of creative ideas to help the environment in other ways, too. Using cloth bags is a wonderful idea. People will save money and help the environment at the same time. There are _____ plastic bags in
                                                                                           3
landfills around the world, and every little bit helps! I also think there are
_____ landfills in this city, so I'm glad the shopping mall plans to
          4
have a recycling center, too. People throw away _____ garbage,
                                                              5
and I hope this will help more people recycle.

I hope you write more articles about the mall.

Sincerely,

Dennis Armstrong

Environmental Student

5 Look at the web post. Then write sentences about what Mi-yon has. Use *not enough* or *too many*.

Thank you, friends! I almost have enough recycled things for my art project, but I still need a few more. If you have any of them, please send them to me at 556 Claremont Street.

	I needed	Now I have	I still need
1. plastic bottles	100	85	15
2. glass bottles	25	30	0
3. plastic bags	250	199	51
4. old lightbulbs	50	40	10
5. old toothbrushes	30	42	0
6. old CDs	175	170	5

Thanks!
Mi-yon Kam, Green Artist

1. *Mi-yon doesn't have enough plastic bottles.*
2. *She has too* _____ .
3. _____
4. _____
5. _____
6. _____

6 Answer the questions with your own information. Use quantifiers.

Example: *Yes, I do. I recycle paper. I could recycle more glass and plastic.* or
No, I don't, and I don't use enough cloth bags.

1. Do you recycle?
2. Do you have recycling bins in your home?
3. Does your town have enough recycling centers?
4. Do you use things in your home to save energy?
5. How much pollution is in your town?
6. How could you make less garbage in your home?

B I'd rather not say.

Complete each conversation with the expressions in the box.

| I'd say about | I'd rather not answer that |

A. Larry: Hi, Kim. How's your new house?

Kim: It's great. We love the solar roof.

Larry: How much is your electric bill now?

Kim: _I'd_____1_____ $40 a month.

Larry: Wow! That's cheap. How much did the solar roof cost?

Kim: _____2_____ , but it was a good purchase. We save money each month, and we help the environment!

| I'd say maybe | I'd rather not say |

B. Alice: Hi, Hala. Where are you going?

Hala: I'm going to the mall.

Alice: What are you going to buy?

Hala: Actually, _____1_____ . It's a surprise for my sister's birthday.

Alice: Oh, OK. Well, I'll see you at her party. What time should I get there?

Hala: Oh, _____2_____ around 6:00 p.m.

Alice: OK.

| probably | I'd prefer not to say |

C. Peng: Wow, Steve. I like your new car.

Steve: Thanks!

Peng: When did you get it?

Steve: Um, _____1_____ about a month ago.

Peng: Is it a hybrid car?

Steve: No, it isn't. The hybrid cars were too expensive.

Peng: Oh, that's too bad. How much do you spend on gas?

Steve: _____2_____ , but definitely too much!

C What will happen?

1 Circle the correct verb to complete each tip for helping the environment.

1. **Use** / Grow / Take a clothesline.
2. **Fix** / Buy / Use leaky faucets.
3. Take / Pay / **Buy** local food.
4. Grow / **Take** / Pay public transportation.
5. **Use** / Pay / Fix rechargeable batteries.
6. Pay / Fix / **Use** cloth shopping bags.
7. **Grow** / Pay / Use your own food.
8. Take / Fix / **Pay** bills online.

2 Look at the pictures. Complete each sentence with the simple present of one tip from Exercise 1.

1. Debbie _uses a clothesline_.

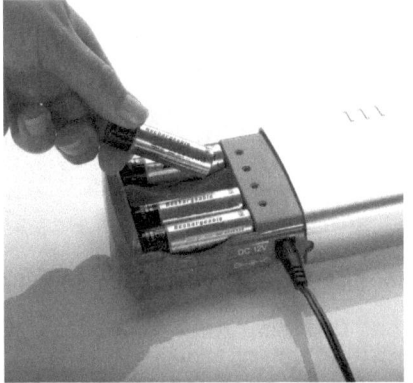
2. Martin _____.

3. Many people in big cities _____.

4. Wesley _____.

5. Rita _____.

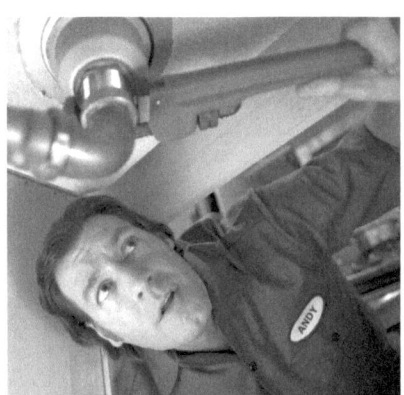
6. Andy _____.

3 Complete the story. Change the main clause of the last sentence to an *if* clause in the next sentence.

1. _If I buy a hybrid car_____, I'll save money on gas.
2. _If I save_____, I'll have more money to spend.
3. _____, I'll buy a new cell phone.
4. _____, I'll recycle my old cell phone.
5. _____, there will be less e-waste.
6. _____, the world will be a better place!

4 Write sentences with the phrases in the chart. Use the first conditional and *will*. Write each sentence two ways.

	Who	The condition	The result
1.	Robert	use rechargeable batteries	buy fewer batteries
2.	Emma	take public transportation	use less gas
3.	Tom and Jackie	have enough money	buy a hybrid car
4.	You	buy local food	get good fruit and vegetables
5.	We	recycle more bottles	help the environment

1. _If Robert uses rechargeable batteries, he'll buy fewer batteries._
   Robert will buy fewer batteries if he uses rechargeable batteries.

2. _____

3. _____

4. _____

5. _____

5 Write the answers to the questions. Use the first conditional and the words in parentheses.

www.ecoblog.cup/Q&A

We want your opinions! Please tell us what you think!

What do you think will happen if more people recycle?

Marc67: _If more people recycle, we might have less garbage_ 1 .
(have less garbage / we / might)

SSGreen: _If more people_ 2 .
(could / help the environment / it)

What do you think will happen if our town starts a wind farm?

EcoJoe: _____3_____ .
(use less energy / we / may)

EvaR22: _____4_____ .
(be more jobs / might / there)

What do you think will happen if the big supermarket closes?

SSGreen: _____5_____ .
(we / may / buy more local food)

EvaR22: _____6_____ .
(some people / get upset / might)

6 Answer the questions with your own opinion. Use *will*, *may*, *might*, or *could*. Use each word at least once.

Example: _If people stop driving cars, there will be less pollution._ or
Many people might lose their jobs if people stop driving cars.

1. What will happen if people stop driving cars? _____
2. What will happen if everyone buys a bike? _____
3. What will happen if we don't have clean water? _____
4. What will happen if people don't fix leaky faucets? _____
5. What will happen if there is no more pollution? _____
6. What will happen if people have to pay for plastic bags in stores? _____
7. What will happen if you grow your own food? _____
8. What will happen if people buy new computers every year? _____

D Finding solutions

1 Read the article. Then check (✓) the chapters that might be in Chelsea Thomson's book.

1. ☐ How to Use Less Energy
2. ☐ How to Waste Time
3. ☐ How to Recycle More
4. ☐ Buy More Than You Need
5. ☐ How to Have More Garbage
6. ☐ How to Use Your Car Less Often
7. ☐ Where to Buy Local Food
8. ☐ Kinds of Food You Can Grow at Home

Dear Readers,

My new book, *Going Completely Green*, is finished! As the title says, I decided to go completely green for a month – no electricity, no running water, no car, no phone, no computer! I didn't even use anything with batteries. It was very difficult, and I decided to write a book about my experience. During the day, I wrote on paper with a pencil. When I wanted to sharpen my pencil, I remembered my pencil sharpener uses electricity. I had to sharpen it with a knife! At night, I used a candle for light. I washed all of my clothes by hand with water from the river behind my house, and then I put them on a clothesline. I walked to a local farm to buy food. I ate mostly fruits and vegetables. I only ate meat about five times, and I cooked it over a fire in my yard. The hardest part was not talking to friends and family on the phone or emailing them. My best friend lives an hour away by car, so I didn't communicate with her at all.

In my opinion, it is impossible to live completely green for a long time, but there are many things you can do. Now, I try to work with the lights off for most of the day. I'm driving my car again, but I try to walk or ride my bike when I only have to go a short distance. I buy more local food now, too. I have to use my computer for work, but I use it for fewer hours each day. I also turn it off when I'm not home. There are many things you can do to use less energy and water. This book will help you learn how to live a greener life. If you follow the steps in my book, you'll really help the environment. Oh, and if you buy my book, you might want to read it by candlelight to save energy!

Chelsea Thomson

2 Read the article again. Rewrite the sentences to correct the underlined mistakes.

1. Chelsea went green for <u>two months</u>.   *Chelsea went green for a month.*
2. She wrote <u>on a computer</u>.   _____
3. She washed her clothes <u>on a clothesline</u>.   _____
4. She thinks it's impossible <u>to work with the lights off</u>.   _____
5. Now she <u>drives her car</u> for short distances.   _____
6. She turns her computer off if <u>she's working</u>.   _____

Relationships

A Healthy relationships

1 Complete the sentences and the puzzle with the correct words. Use words about relationship behaviors.

Across

3. Mr. Jenkins said I didn't do a good job. He always finds things in my work to _____ .

6. Don and Greg _____ all the time. They never listen to each other.

7. Gina is really sorry. She's going to _____ to Kate.

8. Kate knows Gina is sorry. She's going to _____ her.

Down

1. My mother likes to _____ my friends. She always tells me if they are good or bad friends.

2. Please don't _____ . I know you're not being honest.

3. Josh and Dan usually _____ by email, but they sometimes talk on the phone.

4. I want to go to a restaurant, and you want to go to the park. Let's _____ and eat food in the park!

5. Shannon talks about everyone! I hate when people _____ .

Unit 9 Lesson A 65

2 Complete the advice column. Use the infinitive forms of the correct verbs from the box.

| apologize | argue | be | communicate | compromise | ✓lie |

Ask Lee

Dear Lee,

Sometimes it's difficult to tell my parents the truth. I'm a pretty good son, but I make mistakes. I don't want my parents to get upset. I know that it's not good _to lie_₁, but sometimes it's hard to be honest. What's your advice?

– Stressed-Out Son

Dear Stressed-Out Son,

It's not always easy _____₂ honest, but you should try. It's very important _____₃ with your parents. If you say you made a mistake, it might help them understand. They used to be young, and they made mistakes, too.

Dear Lee,

My friends and I are planning a vacation, and we're arguing. Two people want to go to the beach, and one person wants to go hiking. What should we do?

– Ralph

Dear Ralph,

It's never a good idea _____₄ with your friends. It's important _____₅. Why don't you go to a park with mountains near the ocean, like the Manuel Antonio National Park in Costa Rica? You can hike in the mountains and go to the beach!

Dear Lee,

I gossiped about my friend to some other people. I feel terrible, and now she won't talk to me. Please help!

– Pamela G.

Dear Pamela,

When someone is upset with you, it's useful _____₆. If she doesn't want to talk to you, tell her you're sorry in an email. If she knows how you feel, she may forgive you.

66   Unit 9   Lesson A

3 Put the words in the correct order to make a sentence.

1. It's / to help / your neighbors / a good idea / .

   It's a good idea to help your neighbors.

2. to apologize / It's / nice / when you're wrong / .

   _____

3. with your teacher / not good / It's / to argue / .

   _____

4. It's / to compromise / important / with your friends / .

   _____

5. helpful / It's / in class / to listen carefully / .

   _____

6. never a good idea / about your friends / It's / to gossip / .

   _____

4 Complete the sentences with your own ideas. Use expressions from the box.

| It's (not) a good idea | It's (not) helpful | It's (not) useful |
| It's (not) good | It's (not) important | |

Example: **At school:** *It's important to be on time.*

At school:

1. _____ (be) on time.

2. _____ (use) a dictionary in class.

With your friends:

3. _____ (communicate) dishonestly or impatiently.

4. _____ (plan) activities that everyone enjoys.

At a library:

5. _____ (talk) quietly.

6. _____ (write) in the books.

B *I'm really sorry.*

1 Circle the correct phrase to complete each conversation.

A.

Kelly: Hi, Doug. **That's OK** / (**I'm really sorry**)₁ I missed your birthday.

Doug: **There's no need to apologize.** / **I'm sorry.**₂

Kelly: Well, it's not nice to miss a friend's birthday.

Doug: Please, Kelly. **I'm sorry.** / **Don't worry about it.**₃

Kelly: OK. But let's celebrate on Friday.

Doug: Great!

B. **Kelly:** Hi, Doug. **There's no need to apologize** / **I'm sorry**₁, but I can't make it on Friday.

Doug: **That's OK.** / **My apologies.**₂

Kelly: No, it's not. I feel terrible. **My apologies.** / **Don't worry about it.**₃ Can you come over on Saturday? I'll make dinner!

Doug: OK. That sounds great.

2 Complete the conversations. Use some of the expressions from Exercise 1 and your own ideas.

A. **You:** I missed your party. _____1_____ .

Friend: Oh, _____2_____ . What happened?

You: _____3_____ .

Friend: That's too bad.

B. **Friend:** I am very late. _____1_____ .

You: _____2_____ . Is everything all right?

Friend: Not really. _____3_____ .

You: Oh. Too bad!

68   Unit 9   Lesson B

C That can't be the problem.

1 Complete each question with the correct word from the box.

✓ after	into	together
along	on	up
by	on	up

1. Do you take ____after____ anyone in your family? Who?
2. Have you ever been picked _____ in school? By whom?
3. Do you get _____ well with your friends?
4. Have you ever broken _____ with a boyfriend or girlfriend? Who?
5. How often do you get _____ with friends each month? What do you do?
6. Do you like it when friends drop _____ and don't call first? Who does this?
7. Who is the last person you ran _____ when you were shopping?
8. Do you know anyone who is immature and needs to grow _____ ? Who?
9. Who is the person you count _____ the most?

2 Answer the questions in Exercise 1 with your own information. Use phrasal verbs, and add more information when possible.

Example: _Yes, I do. I take after my mother. We're friendly and outgoing. I look like her, too._ or
No, I don't. But I'd like to take after my father. He's really intelligent.

1. _____
2. _____
3. _____
4. _____
5. _____
6. _____
7. _____
8. _____
9. _____

3 Complete the sentences with the correct words from the box.

| can't | may | ✓must |

1. Cindy _____*must*_____ get along well with her family. She's at her parents' house every weekend.

2. I'm not sure, but I think I _____ know where the restaurant is.

3. Mark _____ be breaking up with me! He loves me!

| could | might not | must not |

4. Bev _____ come to work today. She felt sick yesterday.

5. Josh _____ be coming to the party. It started an hour ago, and he's not here.

6. You _____ run into Dan at the mall. I think he's shopping today.

4 Complete the conversation with *must*, *can't*, or *might*.

Sandra: Good morning, Paul. Do you know where Dan is? I didn't see his car outside.

Paul: I'm not sure. He _____*might*_____ be at a doctor's appointment.

Sandra: No, he _____2_____ have a doctor's appointment today. I have all his appointments in my calendar.

Paul: You're right. He _____3_____ be taking the bus today. The buses are often late.

Sandra: Well, he _____4_____ have a good reason. He's never late.

Paul: Wait! My phone's ringing. It _____5_____ be Dan. Let me see. . . . No. It _____6_____ be Dan. It's not his number.

Sandra: Well, you should answer it! Dan _____7_____ be calling from a different phone if there's a problem.

A minute later . . .

Paul: Yes. It was Dan. He _____8_____ be feeling pretty stressed. He ran out of gas and had to ask a stranger to drive him to a gas station. But he left his cell phone in his car, so he had to ask the stranger to use her phone.

70   Unit 9   Lesson C

5 Answer the questions with your own ideas. Use words from the box to speculate and to say how sure you are.

| can't could may (not) might (not) must (not) |

Example: *I don't know. She might be looking for some money.* or
I see her car. She must be looking for her keys.

1. What is the woman looking for?

_____

2. What animal is it?

_____

3. Why is the boy crying?

_____

4. Why are they arguing?

_____

5. Why is the woman late?

_____

6. Where are they going?

_____

D Getting advice

1 Read the advice. Who is the speaker giving the advice to? Write the correct heading from the magazine article.

1. "I'm sorry, but you need to get more organized. Your work is often late."   _To a co-worker_

2. "It must feel bad that James doesn't want to play with you. Could you ask Kahil?"   _____

3. "I don't think he's good for you. Do you ever think about breaking up?"   _____

How to Give Advice

Everyone has an opinion, but sometimes it's not easy to give advice. This is really true for important relationships. Here are some tips on how you can give advice in different relationships.

To a child If you aren't careful, children might get angry when you give them advice. They are often immature, and they don't understand that you want to help. It's useful to tell them you understand what they are going through before you give them advice. Be considerate, think about how they might feel, and remember that their opinions matter. It's not helpful to speak loudly or to criticize; this makes children feel worse, and they might not listen to you.

To a co-worker It can be difficult to give advice to people at work, so it's often good to apologize first. For example, say, "I'm sorry, but I think you could . . ." And remember that it's never a good idea to judge people. Give advice about what you think should change about the person's work, not about the person! Also remember that in work situations, you often have to compromise. You may give advice, but the person might not take it!

To a friend Friends can be the hardest people to give advice to. It's important to be honest, but you should also be kind. When you give advice to a friend, don't argue. Try to communicate with your friend. Ask questions and really understand your friend's problem before you give advice.

These tips are useful in other types of relationships, too. The important thing to remember is to be patient with others, and give them a chance to respond to your advice. It's also helpful to give advice when the person is ready to listen. Don't give advice when the person is extremely upset or stressed. Try to find a time when he or she is more relaxed.

2 Read the article again. Check (✓) what the writer says about giving advice.

1. Don't argue. ✓
2. You may need to compromise. ☐
3. You might need to get angry. ☐
4. Be honest. ☐
5. Don't give advice about work. ☐
6. Ask questions. ☐

72   Unit 9   Lesson D

Living your life

unit 10

A He taught himself.

1 Complete the puzzle with words for qualities for success. What's the mystery word?

1. a strong interest in something
2. the quality of showing no fear
3. the ability to change easily
4. a commitment to something
5. the belief that you can succeed
6. the ability to develop original ideas

| | ¹E | N | T | H | U | S | I | A | S | M |

2 Circle the correct words to complete the article.

Man Saves Friend

Farmers Jim Rolland and Ryan Jensen were trying to take soybeans out of a large bin, but they wouldn't come out. Jim Rolland was **(confident)** / **confidence** that he could fix the problem, but his **confident** / **confidence** got him in trouble. He climbed some stairs and went into the bin. The beans moved and covered him completely!

Ryan Jensen told another worker to call for help. Then he had a **creative** / **creativity** idea. He wasn't sure it was **wise** / **wisdom**, but he also went into the bin. He got on his stomach on top of the beans. For four hours, he moved beans so Rolland could breathe. His **dedicated** / **dedication** and **brave** / **bravery** saved his friend's life.

Rescue workers finally came. They removed the beans and helped Rolland out of the bin. He was fine, and he was happy to have **talented** / **talent** people help him.

3 Put the words in the correct order to make sentences.

1. a picture of / art class / myself / I / painted / in / .
   I painted a picture of myself in art class.

2. by / The / isn't / itself / computer / going to work / .
   _____

3. brave / herself / doesn't / mother / My / consider / .
   _____

4. Japanese / themselves / taught / Kyle / and Mick / .
   _____

5. blame / Don't / for / my / yourselves / problems / !
   _____

6. did / Chris / When / hurt / himself / ?
   _____

7. yourself / by / draw / Did / you / that picture / ?
   _____

8. enjoyed / We / on / ourselves / trip to New York / our / .
   _____

4 Complete the sentences with the correct reflexive pronouns.

What do people like to do by _____**themselves**_____ ? Here's what some
                                        1
of our readers said:

- I like to travel by _____ . I always meet interesting people,
                              2
  and sometimes they teach me words of wisdom. (Tom P., Chicago)

- My brother and I love to play video games by _____ .
                                                          3
  We don't like our sisters to play with us. (Jake M., San Antonio)

- My husband likes to cook by _____ . And that's OK with
                                        4
  me! (Lidia S., Boston)

- My daughter is very enthusiastic, and she likes to do extreme sports by
  _____ . It makes me nervous! (Na-young K., San Francisco)
             5

What do you like to do by _____ ?
                                     6

5 Complete the conversations with the correct personal and reflexive pronouns.

A. **Rachel:** _____I_____ like your scarf, Phoebe.

   Phoebe: Thanks. I made it by _____2_____ .

   Rachel: Wow. _____3_____ have a lot of talent!

B. **Sheila:** Look! My son painted this by _____1_____ .

   Feng: _____2_____ did a great job.

C. **Joe:** Did you hear what happened to Emily?

   Martin: No, _____1_____ didn't.

   Joe: She hurt _____2_____ skiing.

   Martin: Is _____3_____ OK?

   Joe: Yes, she is.

D. **Laura:** We really enjoyed _____1_____ at your party, Pedro.

   Pedro: I'm glad _____2_____ had fun, but the food I made was terrible.

   Laura: Don't blame _____3_____ . It was fine.

   Pedro: You're right. My friends enjoyed _____4_____ . That's what counts!

6 Answer the questions with your own information.

Example: <u>*Yes, I do. I'm very enthusiastic about good music.*</u> or

         <u>*No, I don't. I'm not enthusiastic about anything.*</u>

1. Do you consider yourself enthusiastic? What are you enthusiastic about? _____

2. Do you consider yourself flexible, or do you like to do things your own way? _____

3. What do you like to do by yourself? _____

4. Have you ever painted yourself? What did the picture look like? _____

5. Do you know someone who hurt himself or herself playing a sport? What happened? _____

6. Do you think people should travel by themselves? Why or why not? _____

B I'll give it some thought.

1 Write the conversation in the correct order.

> Their prices are really high. You should go to Comp.com. It's an online store.
> ✓ Hi, Tina. Where are you going?
> Hmm. . . . I'll give it some thought. Thanks.
> I don't think you should do that.
> I'm going to Tech-It to buy a new computer.
> Really? Why not?

Erin: _Hi, Tina. Where are you going?_

Tina: _____

Erin: _____

Tina: _____

Erin: _____

Tina: _____

2 Complete the conversations. Use information from the pictures and sentences from the box. Use Exercise 1 as a model. Sometimes more than one answer is possible.

> I wouldn't recommend that.   I'll think about it.
> I'll see.   I'm not sure that's the best idea.

1. **Ed:** Hi, Ali. Where are you going?

   Ali: I'm going to _____ to buy a new _____ .

   Ed: _____ .

   Ali: Really? _____ ?

   Ed: Their prices are really high. You should go to _____ . It's an _____ store.

   Ali: Hmm. . . . _____ . Thanks.

2. **Sasha:** Hi, Marc. _____ ?

   Marc: I'm going to _____ .

   Sasha: _____ .

   Marc: Really? _____ ?

   Sasha: Their prices are really high. _____ .

   Marc: Hmm. . . . _____ . Thanks.

C What would you do?

1 Rewrite the sentences. Change the underlined words. Use the phrasal verb in parentheses and the correct pronoun.

1. Can you show me where Linda is? (point out)
   Can you point her out?

2. You need to do your homework again. It has a lot of mistakes. (do over)

3. I didn't accept that job. (turn down)

4. I'm going to donate these shirts. (give away)

5. Please don't mention his daughter. (bring up)

6. When are you going to return the money I lent you? (pay back)

7. We really should discuss our problem. (talk over)

8. Can I use this computer before I buy it? (try out)

9. I'll return your camera tomorrow, if that's OK. (give back)

10. Let's do the conference call later. (put off)

2 Complete Bianca's email with the correct forms of the verbs in parentheses. Use the second conditional.

To: RobbieJ@cup.org
From: Bianca54@cup.com
Subject: What would you do?

Hi Rob,

I have some interesting news. My aunt might give me some money! I _would do_ (1) (do) so many things if I _____ (2) (have) a lot of money. If I _____ (3) (be) rich, I _____ (4) (not work) anymore! That would be great. If I _____ (5) (not have) a job, I _____ (6) (travel) around the world. I _____ (7) (feel) very lucky if I _____ (8) (get) a lot of money. What would you do?

Your friend,

Bianca

3 Now complete Rob's email with the correct forms of the verbs in parentheses. Use the second conditional.

To: Bianca54@cup.com
From: RobbieJ@cup.org
Subject: RE: What would you do?

Hey Bianca!

Wow! It _would be_ (1) (be) great if your aunt _____ (2) (give) you money. Is it a lot of money? If I _____ (3) (have) a lot of money, I _____ (4) (make) a big, beautiful garden. But I can't have a garden at my apartment, so I _____ (5) (need) a house with a big yard. I _____ (6) (use) a lot of my money to buy a house, and there _____ (7) (be) a lot of room for two big gardens: a vegetable garden and a flower garden. I _____ (8) (give) some money to my brother, too, if I _____ (9) (be) rich. He _____ (10) (not have to pay) me back.

Take care,

Rob

78 Unit 10 Lesson C

4 Write questions with the words in parentheses. Use the second conditional.

1. (What / you / do / if / you / be / braver)
   <u>What would you do if you were braver?</u>
2. (What / you / buy / for your friends / if / you / have / a lot of money)
   _____
3. (Where / you / go / if / you / have / a free ticket)
   _____
4. (What / you / do / if / you / have / 200 vacation days)
   _____
5. (What instrument / you / play / if / you and your friends / have / a band)
   _____
6. (What sport / you / try / if / you / try / an extreme sport)
   _____
7. (What / you / give away / if / you / move)
   _____

5 Answer the questions in Exercise 4 with your own information.

Example: <u>If I were braver, I would take a trip around the world by myself.</u>

1. _____
2. _____
3. _____
4. _____
5. _____
6. _____
7. _____

D What an accomplishment!

1 Read the letter. Then circle the correct answers.

1. How old is Thomas?   99   100   101
2. Who is Peter?   his brother   his son   his grandson

Dear Peter,

Can you believe I'll be 100 years old next week? If I had a dollar for every great thing I did, I would be rich! I decided to write to you about a few important things that happened in each decade of my life.

1920s – These are the first years I really remember. Jazz music was extremely popular, and I was in a jazz band. We were very dedicated to our music!

1930s – Many people didn't have a lot of money in the 1930s, but I worked very hard. In 1937, I bought myself a car! If I had that car today, it would be worth a lot of money!

1940s – This was a sad decade because of World War II, but the 1940s were also happy for me in many ways. I met your grandmother in 1941 when I was a soldier. A friend pointed her out to me at the supermarket. We got married two years later. That was a wise decision! Your mother was born in 1944.

1950s – We bought our first TV. I remember trying it out in the store first. It was amazing! And with the Civil Rights Movement starting, it was a good time to have a TV.

1960s – This was a very creative time in my life. Your grandmother was painting, and I started taking pictures. In 1969, a man walked on the moon!

1970s – I was offered a promotion in 1972, but I turned it down. I retired six years later.

1980s – I started a volunteer program at a hospital in 1982 and was busy with that for several years.

1990s – In 1995, a park in our town was dedicated to me for the volunteer work I did at the hospital. Do you remember when you bought me a computer in 1997? I never taught myself how to use it!

2000s – The 2000s were a quiet decade, but I've had a lot of time to spend with family. I bought a cell phone this year, but I took it back. I didn't think I really needed it. I guess I'm a little old-fashioned!

See you next week for my birthday!

Your grandfather,

Thomas O'Malley

---

2 Read the letter again. Then number the events in the correct order.

_____ He turned down a promotion.   _____ He got a cell phone.

_____ He got married.   _____ He bought a car.

_____ He started a volunteer program.   _____ He started taking pictures.

__1__ He was in a jazz band.   _____ He got a computer.

80   Unit 10   Lesson D

Music

A Music trivia

1 Put the words in the correct order to make phrases about music. Add hyphens, if necessary.

1. best / artist / selling — *best-selling artist*
2. video / winning / award _____
3. performer / often / downloaded _____
4. priced / high / ticket _____
5. group / named / oddly _____
6. singers / well / known _____
7. breaking / hit / record _____
8. nice / voice / sounding _____

2 Complete the webpage with the phrases from Exercise 1.

Jake and Jill's Music Awards

Hello fans! Here's today's music news from your favorite music fans!

- Sting, a *best-selling artist*₁ from the 1980s, and his wife started the Rainforest Concert in 1991. They have the concert every two years. This year, _____₂ , like Elton John and Bruce Springsteen, performed. Tickets were $2,500 or more! That's a _____₃ , but all of the money helps save rain forests around the world.

- Listen to *Yellow Fever!* It's a great album by Señor Coconut and His Orchestra. Yes, this is a very _____₄ (*señor* is a Spanish word, but Señor Coconut is actually German), but we think each singer has a very _____₅ !

- Who is the most _____₆ on our website? Taylor Swift! Her song "Love Story" has been downloaded over 4 million times, and the video won the Country Music Association Award for Best Music Video in 2009. To listen to her _____₇ , *click here*. To watch her _____₈ , *click here*.

3 Complete the sentences with the correct forms of the words in parentheses. Use the past passive.

We Are the World

Kenny Rogers and Lionel Richie

"We Are the World" <u>was recorded</u> (record) in 1985. The money it made _____ (give) to groups that help hungry people in Africa. The song _____ (write) by Michael Jackson and Lionel Richie. Many famous singers, like Kenny Rogers, Bob Dylan, and Stevie Wonder, _____ (ask) to sing it.

A video _____ (make) while the singers were recording the song. The song and video _____ (play) on TV in the spring of 1985.

In 2010, "We Are the World" _____ (record) again with new singers to help the people of Haiti. The song _____ (sing) by over 80 well-known musicians, like Justin Bieber and Jennifer Hudson. It _____ (see) on TV by many people on February 12.

4 Rewrite each sentence in the past passive. If there is information about who did the action, use a *by* phrase.

1. Four men planned the Woodstock Festival in 1969.

   <u>The Woodstock Festival was planned by four men in 1969.</u>

2. Someone asked many well-known singers to sing at Woodstock.

   _____

3. Someone gave information about the festival on the radio.

   _____

4. Someone allowed about 400,000 to 500,000 music fans into the festival.

   _____

5. People made a documentary about Woodstock in 1970.

   _____

6. *Rolling Stone* magazine listed Woodstock as one of "50 Moments that Changed the History of Rock and Roll."

   _____

5 Look at the chart of some record-breaking hits. Then answer the questions. Use the past passive.

Song	Singer(s)	Year of release	Millions of recordings sold
Candle in the Wind	Elton John	1997	37
White Christmas	Bing Crosby	1942	30
We Are the World	Many musicians	1985	20
Rock Around the Clock	Bill Haley and his Comets	1954	17
I Want to Hold Your Hand	The Beatles	1963	12
Hey Jude	The Beatles	1968	10
It's Now or Never	Elvis Presley	1960	10
I Will Always Love You	Whitney Houston	1992	10

1. Who was "It's Now or Never" sung by?   _It was sung by Elvis Presley._
2. When was "White Christmas" released?   _____
3. Who were "I Want to Hold Your Hand" and "Hey Jude" sung by?   _____
4. How many recordings of "We Are the World" were sold?   _____
5. What song was released in 1954?   _____
6. What song was sung by Elton John?   _____
7. How many recordings of "I Will Always Love You" were sold?   _____
8. When was "Hey Jude" released?   _____

6 Answer the questions with your own information. Write complete sentences.

Example: _My favorite song was "Candle in the Wind."_

1. What was your favorite song when you were 12?   _____
2. Who was it sung by?   _____
3. What kind of music was it?   _____
4. Was a video made of the song? What was it like?   _____
5. Was the singer or group well known?   _____
6. Is the singer or group well known today?   _____
7. Did you ever go to a concert of the singer or group? Where was it?   _____
8. Was a documentary ever made about the singer or group? What was it called?   _____

B The first thing you do is . . .

Rewrite the instructions. Use the words in the box.

A.
> **How to Buy a Song**
> 1. Find the song you want, and click on it.
> 2. Enter your credit card number.
> 3. Read the information, and click "Yes."

| After that | ✓First | To finish |

How to Buy a Song

First, find the song you want, and click on it.
_____
_____

B.
> **How to Listen to Music on Your Phone**
> 1. Open your music program.
> 2. Choose the song you want to listen to.
> 3. Click "Play."

| The last thing you do is | Then | To start |

How to Listen to Music on Your Phone

_____
_____
_____

C.
> **How to Record Your Voice**
> 1. Put the recorder near you.
> 2. Hit the "Record" button.
> 3. Sing a song or speak into the recorder.

| Finally | Next | The first thing you do is |

How to Record Your Voice

_____
_____
_____

C Music and me

1 Complete the sentences and the puzzle with the correct verbs.

Across

1. My favorite band will _____ a new album next week.
5. Justin Bieber sang the song "My World," but he didn't _____ it. Usher was one of the producers.
7. Coldplay will _____ their tour dates on their website.
8. Beethoven couldn't hear anything, but he was able to _____ great music. Many people listen to his music today, almost 200 years after he died.

Down

2. Lady Gaga likes to _____ her audience in her concerts.
3. I can't sing very well, but I really _____ music. I listen to it all the time.
4. Do you know when your brother's band is going to _____ their new song? I really would like to go see his band.
6. We're going to _____ our new song in the studio next week. They have new computers we can use.

2 Circle the correct word to complete each sentence.

1. Beethoven's Fifth Symphony is my favorite musical **compose** / **(composition)**.
2. My favorite band **released** / **a release** a new album yesterday.
3. My uncle **produces** / **production** songs, but he can't sing or play an instrument.
4. Jonathan found one of his father's old **record** / **recordings**.
5. Wendy loves to go to **perform** / **performances** at music festivals.
6. My sister likes to **entertain** / **entertainment** our family.
7. The band made an **announce** / **announcement** about their tour yesterday.
8. What time does the **produce** / **production** of *Hamlet* start?

3 Answer the questions with your own information. Write complete sentences.

Example: <u>My favorite kind of entertainment is the movies.</u>

1. What's your favorite kind of entertainment? _____
2. Have you ever taken a music class? When? _____
3. Have you ever heard your favorite singer perform? Where? _____
4. Have you ever been to a party for an album release? Where? _____
5. What kind of music do you appreciate? _____

4 Complete the email with *yet* or *already*.

To: Lee1988@cup.org
From: JJJ@cup.com
Subject: Do you have plans on Friday night?

Hey Lee!

Have you made plans for Friday night ____yet____(1)? My brother's band, Time Travel, is playing at the Music Café. I've _____(2) seen them about ten times, and they're great! Have you listened to the CD I sent you _____(3)? I've _____(4) bought tickets for my sister and me, but I haven't gotten a ticket for you _____(5). Let me know if you want to go. Tickets aren't high-priced. They're only $10. Time Travel has _____(6) started recording their next CD. It hasn't been released _____(7), but they might play a few songs from it on Friday. I hope you can come!

Jay

5 Look at Carla's To-Do list. Then write sentences about what she has and hasn't done. Use the present perfect with *yet* or *already*.

> To Do
> Send Jen and Sandra information about the Coldplay concert ✓
> Call Sandra and Jen about tickets to see Coldplay ✓
> Buy the tickets ✓
> Clean the house
> Go to the airport to pick up Jen and Sandra

1. Carla has already sent Jen and Sandra information about the Coldplay concert.
2. She _____
3. _____
4. _____
5. _____

6 Look at Jen and Sandra's To-Do list. Then write questions and answers about what they have and haven't done. Use the present perfect with *yet* or *already*.

> To Do
> Do the laundry ✓
> Clean the apartment ✓
> Listen to Coldplay's new songs
> Give our parents Carla's cell phone number ✓
> Pay Carla for the tickets

1. Question: Have Jen and Sandra done the laundry yet?
   Answer: Yes, they have already done the laundry.
2. Q: Have they _____
   A: _____
3. Q: _____
   A: _____
4. Q: _____
   A: _____
5. Q: _____
   A: _____

D Thoughts on music

1 Read the article. Then write why musicians don't want people to give music to their friends.

_____

Music Laws

Today, many people get their music from the Internet. But is it legal? It depends on how you get the music and what country you live in. It's sometimes OK, but it's often against the law.

It is usually legal to buy songs from websites on the Internet. If you buy a song, you can make a copy for yourself. However, in the United States and some other countries, it is illegal to make copies of the song for your friends. This is because laws protect people's ideas and work. If everyone copied and gave music to their friends, people would not buy the singers' albums, and musicians couldn't make money for their work.

Also, in many countries it's illegal to *bootleg* music. This is a word that describes when people go to a live performance, record the music, and then upload the music to the Internet to give to their friends or to sell. Sometimes at concerts musicians perform new songs before they are recorded in a studio. They don't want their music released on the Internet before their albums are sold.

Some people *sample* music when they compose songs. This means they use a part of someone else's song in their music. This is often done in hip-hop music. Sampling is usually legal if you have permission from the singer, but it is usually not OK to use someone else's music without permission.

Interesting Music Trivia

- In 1990, part of a David Bowie song was sampled by Vanilla Ice without permission. After the song was released, Vanilla Ice had to pay David Bowie a lot of money for using his music.

- In 1999, Napster was created as a way to get music from friends without paying for it on the Internet. Napster had to stop doing this in the United States, and now people have to pay for the music.

2 Read the article. Then write L (legal – OK) or I (illegal – not OK) for these actions according to the laws in the United States.

1. You can buy songs on the Internet from websites. __L__

2. You can get a song for free from a friend. _____

3. You can bootleg music from a live performance. _____

4. You can sample music without permission. _____

On vacation

A Travel preferences

1 Complete the travel ads with the correct phrases from the box.

| buy handicrafts | listen to live music | ✓ speak a foreign language | visit landmarks |
| go to clubs | see wildlife | try local food | volunteer |

European Vacation

Can you _speak a foreign language_ ?
If you speak French, Spanish, or Portuguese, this is the vacation for you! Visit France, Spain, and Portugal. _____2_____, like the Eiffel Tower in France and famous museums in Spain, or stay near the ocean in Portugal.

Miami Dream

The weather is wonderful in Miami for most of the year. Visit beaches during the day. At night, _____5_____ to dance! There are also many places to _____6_____. You can go to a concert or listen to free music in the parks or even on the beach.

South American Working Vacation

Visit Peru and Ecuador in a different way. _____3_____ your time to help people and animals. First, teach English in Peru, and then work in the Amazon rain forest. You'll _____4_____, like frogs, river dolphins, and monkeys.

Seoul Markets

Do you like shopping? Tour Seoul's markets. Namdaemun is the largest market in Seoul, and it sells many different things. You can _____7_____, like bags and jewelry. You can even _____8_____ while you are shopping at the market or take some home to cook.

Unit 12 Lesson A 89

2

Put the words in the correct order to make sentences. Make one of the words a gerund. Use the simple present forms of the other verbs.

1. be / by boat / Travel / very slow

   Traveling by boat is very slow.

2. enjoy / I / foreign languages / speak / when I travel

   _____

3. buy / handicrafts for my cousins / I / in local markets / like

   _____

4. be / to cook / I / interested in / learn / Thai food

   _____

5. be / to do on vacation / landmarks / my favorite thing / Visit

   _____

6. be / concerned about / help / I / wildlife in the ocean

   _____

3

Complete the conversation with the gerund forms of the correct words from the box.

| go | ✓hike | travel | volunteer | volunteer |

Mark: Hey, Jesse. Where are you going for vacation?

Jesse: I don't know. I enjoy _____*hiking*_____ in the mountains. Any suggestions?
                                    1

Mark: How about the Rockies in Canada?

Jesse: I don't think so. I prefer _____ somewhere warm.
                                              2

Mark: Why don't you go to Costa Rica? There are mountains there, and it's warm.

Jesse: That's a good idea. You know, I'm interested in _____ .
                                                                    3
Maybe I could help animals there.

Mark: _____ is a great idea. It should make the vacation cheaper,
              4
too. Are you going by yourself?

Jesse: No, I'm not. I dislike _____ alone. I'm going with friends.
                                          5

4 Look at the chart. Then complete the sentences.

Name	Travel activity	Opinion	Preference
Cara	travel / by bus	slow	go / by train
Diego	drive / a car	dangerous	ride / a bike
Donna and Nicole	visit / landmarks	boring	see / wildlife
Tom	go / to clubs	not fun	go / to concerts
Ian and Meg	travel / by plane	expensive	stay / home
Libby	learn / Chinese	difficult	study / Spanish

1. Cara thinks _traveling by bus is slow_. She prefers _going by train_.
2. Diego thinks _____. He _____.
3. Donna and Nicole think _____. They _____.
4. Tom thinks _____. He _____.
5. Ian and Meg _____. They _____.
6. Libby _____. She _____.

5 Answer the questions with your own information. Use gerunds when possible.

Example: _I'm interested in buying handicrafts and trying local food._

1. What vacation activities are you interested in? _____
2. What do you enjoy doing on vacation? _____
3. What do you dislike doing on vacation? _____
4. What do you think is the easiest way to travel? _____
5. What do you think is the cheapest way to travel? _____
6. What do you dislike about planning a vacation? _____
7. What are you concerned about when looking for a hotel? _____
8. What do you worry about when you travel? _____
9. Do you like listening to live local music when you travel? What kind? _____
10. Are you interested in writing about your vacations? Why or why not? _____

B Don't forget to . . .

Complete the conversations with sentences from the box.

> Don't forget to get to the station 20 minutes early.
> Let me remind you to get there before 8:00 p.m.
> Remember to look for plane tickets today.
> ✓Would you like a bus ticket or a train ticket?
> Would you prefer one bed or two beds?
> Would you rather go to a warm place or a cold place?

A. **Mr. Harris:** Hello. Can I help you?

Richard: Yes. I'd like a ticket for Chicago, please.

Mr. Harris: OK. _Would you like a bus ticket or a train ticket_ ?

Richard: Oh, well, which one is better?

Mr. Harris: The bus takes longer, but it's cheaper.

Richard: Hmm. . . . I'll take the bus. I'm going on Saturday morning.

Mr. Harris: Good. A bus leaves at 9:15. _____ 2 _____ .

Richard: OK. Thanks.

B. **Blanca:** Hey, Erica. _____ 1 _____ .

Erica: Oh, yeah. Thanks. I'll look for the best tickets online after work. _____ 2 _____ ?

Blanca: Let's go somewhere hot, like the beach.

Erica: OK. I'll look for some cheap tickets, and we can make plans tonight.

Blanca: Great. Thanks.

C. **Ms. Ito:** Can I help you?

Shan: Yes, I need a room for three nights.

Ms. Ito: No problem. _____ 1 _____ ?

Shan: One bed, please. Oh, and is there a restaurant in this hotel?

Ms. Ito: Yes, there is. It's right over there. _____ 2 _____ . It closes at 8:30.

92   Unit 12   Lesson B

C Rules and recommendations

1 Complete the words for the extreme sports.

1. p_aragliding_
2. r_____
   c_____
3. b_____
   j_____
4. w_____ -
   w_____
   r_____
5. k_____
   s_____
6. w_____
7. s_____
8. s_____

Unit 12   Lesson C   93

2 Circle the correct expression to complete each sentence.

1. **Necessity:** _____ fill out this form before you go paragliding.
   a. You don't have to   (b.) You must   c. You'd better

2. **Recommendation:** Sandra _____ plan her vacation before she goes.
   a. doesn't have to   b. must   c. ought to

3. **Lack of necessity:** You _____ wear warm clothes when rock climbing in the summer.
   a. don't have to   b. have to   c. shouldn't

4. **Necessity:** Nancy and Carol _____ wear heavy boots when they go snowboarding.
   a. should   b. shouldn't   c. have to

5. **Recommendation:** _____ take sunglasses when you go white-water rafting.
   a. You must   b. You've got to   c. You'd better

6. **Lack of necessity:** Jorge _____ go skydiving if he doesn't want to.
   a. has to   b. doesn't have to   c. shouldn't

7. **Necessity:** _____ pay for my kite surfing lessons before I can take the first lesson.
   a. I've got to   b. I don't have to   c. I'd better

8. **Recommendation:** Sue and Teddy _____ go bungee jumping. It's very dangerous.
   a. don't have to   b. have got to   c. shouldn't

3 Complete the article with *must* or *should*.

✈ How to Get to Your Flight Faster

Airports have a lot of rules. Here are some tips to help you get through the airport faster.

- You ___*should*___ print your boarding pass at home, if possible.
  1

- You _____ get to the airport early. It's a good
  2
  idea to arrive an hour before your flight.

- You _____ have your passport or other ID.
  3
  You can't get on the plane without one of them.

- You _____ take off your shoes at security.
  4
  They won't let you go through with them on.

- You _____ wear shoes that are easy to take off.
  5
  You'll move faster.

Airport Security

4 Circle the correct words to complete the instructions.

Welcome to the Riverside Park white-water rafting trip. We want you to have a safe trip, so there are a few things that you **(have to)** / **don't have to** do.¹ First of all, **you'd better** / **you shouldn't**² listen to your guide. That's me, so please listen to me carefully. Now for the safety rules: **You must not** / **You must**³ sit on the raft at all times. Stand only when you are getting on or off the raft. And while we are riding, you **don't have to** / **ought to**⁴ hold on to the raft.

It's going to be warm today, so you **don't have to** / **must**⁵ wear a coat, but you **should** / **shouldn't**⁶ wear a hat. It will protect your skin and eyes from the sun. Later we'll stop at a beach and have lunch there. **You shouldn't** / **You'd better**⁷ eat on the raft. Finally, don't forget that rafting can be dangerous. **You don't have to** / **You've got to**⁸ be careful all day. If you follow my instructions, you'll be safe and have fun!

5 Write your own rules and recommendations for each place. Use modals for necessity, lack of necessity, and recommendations.

Example: In a restaurant: 1. *You must pay for your food.*
2. *You don't have to eat something you don't like.*
3. *You should leave a little extra money for the waiter or waitress.*

In a restaurant:

1. _____
2. _____
3. _____

At the movies:

4. _____
5. _____
6. _____

In your classroom:

7. _____
8. _____
9. _____

D Seeing the sights

1 Read the catalogue page. Then number the pictures to match the descriptions.

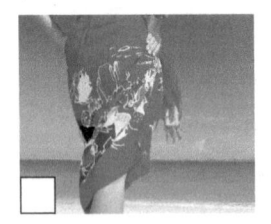

☐ (sarong) ☐ (binoculars) ☐ (bag) ☐ (camera) ☐ (earplugs)

World Tour — The Catalogue for Travelers

Every year, World Tour chooses the top five items every traveler must have. Read about what you should buy this year.

1. Digi-2300 Camera $129.99
Every traveler ought to have a good, reliable digital camera. We recommend the Digi-2300. It's small, so you can easily take it anywhere. It's great for taking pictures of landmarks or just for taking pictures of your friends. It's a reasonable price, and it takes great pictures.

2. XP Binoculars $52.99
Look through these fantastic binoculars to see wildlife on your next safari. Using them is a great way to see animals safely and up close. They make the animals look ten times larger. You can also use these binoculars underwater, so they're great for looking at fish, too. They will fit easily in your bag because they're very small. Put them in your bag next to your new camera!

To order, call (800) 555-3400 or visit our website at www.worldtour.com/cup

3. Simple Sarong $18.50
Sarongs are very useful, and there's one size for everyone. Women can use sarongs as a skirt or a dress, but men can use them, too. They work well as towels for the beach or to use after swimming, waterskiing, and kite surfing. Dry your body off, and then the towel dries in minutes! Get it in blue, black, red, orange, or green.

4. Earplugs   2 for $3.50
Earplugs are a cheap and practical gift for a friend or for yourself. Traveling on airplanes, buses, and trains can be noisy, but you won't hear any noise with these earplugs. Put them in your ears and fall asleep!

5. The "It Bag" $75.00
Our best bag is called the "It Bag" because you have to have it! It can be small or large because it's expandable. It's perfect for a day trip or for a weekend vacation. Get it in black, brown, or red.

2 Read the catalogue page again. Then write T (true), F (false), or NI (no information).

1. The binoculars are cheaper than the camera. __T__
2. The camera only comes in one color. _____
3. You have to wear the sarong. _____
4. The earplugs aren't expensive. _____
5. Expanding the bag is easy. _____